The Events List

By Latricia Bradley

DEDICATION

This book is dedicated to my family,
friends and colleagues.

I would like to thank God
for giving me the vision to write this book.

"I can do all things through Christ
which strengthen me." Phil 4:13

TABLE OF CONTENTS

1) INTRODUCTION

"Would you like to plan your own event; however, you are not sure where to begin? Planning an event can become stressful and overpowering. This guide has been developed to help you through the course of planning a successful event. It delivers a step-by-step process to keep you organized with a checklist and helpful hints in planning your event from beginning to end." So let's get started!

2) THE EVENTS LIST

1. Purpose of the event
2. Vision of the event
3. Create your budget
4. Select a date and time
5. Make your guest list
6. Select a venue
7. Create a seating chart
8. List rental items needed
9. Advertise your event
10. Mail invitations
11. Decide on your menu
12. Hire a baker
13. Décor (style/purchases)
14. Hire a photographer/videographer
15. Decide on event attire
16. Entertainment
17. Transportation
18. Complete a timeline and itinerary for the event

After deciding what you will need for your event, you will need to set a time-line in order to complete your tasks.

We are providing you with an example of a twelve-month timeline and budget. However, adjust accordingly.

3) TIMELINE

12 months
- Determine the purpose of your event
- Determine style and color
- Set a date
- Set a budget
- Compile guest list
- Book venue
- Advertise
- Recruit family or friends to assist you with coordinating the event

9-11 months
- Send out save-the-date cards
- Book caterer
- Book entertainment
- Book florist
- Book photographer and videographer

6-8 months
- Determine your menu
- Book cake baker
- Book transportation

4-5 months

- Order invitations
- Hire a calligrapher
- Reserve rental equipment

3 months

- Finalize guest list
- Mail out invitations

1-2 months

- Order favors
- Finalize floral proposal

1-2 weeks

- Call guests who haven't RSVP'd
- Call location manager and make sure your vendors have access to the site when they need it
- Finalize seating chart and give it to the site manager
- Check in with all vendors and confirm all details
- Assemble or package favors

3-7 days

- Finalize all transportation details
- Set aside tips for your vendors

Day of Event

- Provide your coordinators with the timeline, itinerary and vendors list
- Eat a small meal in the morning
- Enjoy your day!

After the Ceremony

- Mail thank you cards

4) BUDGET

Venue, Food & Beverage 45%

Décor & Flowers 20%

Photography and Videography 14%

Entertainment 5%

Rentals 5%

Stationery 4%

Transportation and Accommodations 4%

Miscellaneous 3%

5) HELPFUL TIPS – PLACE SETTINGS

FORMAL PLACE SETTING

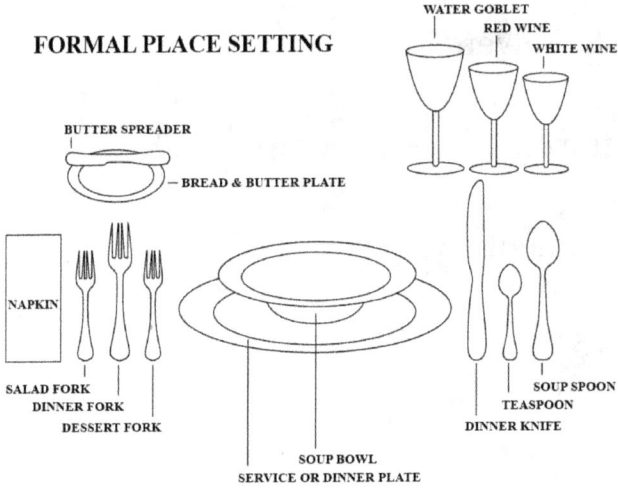

WATER GOBLET
RED WINE
WHITE WINE

BUTTER SPREADER

BREAD & BUTTER PLATE

NAPKIN

SALAD FORK
DINNER FORK
DESSERT FORK

SOUP BOWL
SERVICE OR DINNER PLATE

SOUP SPOON
TEASPOON
DINNER KNIFE

INFORMAL PLACE SETTING

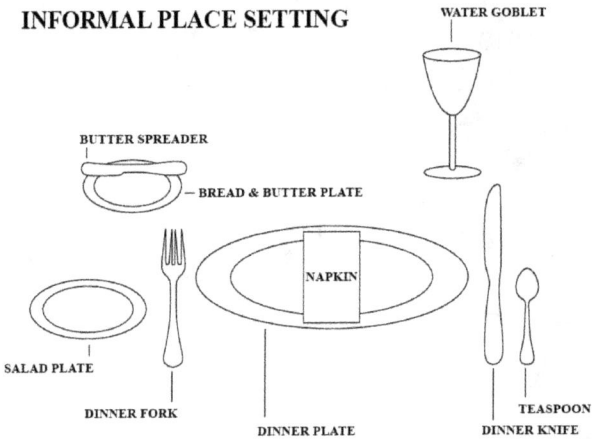

WATER GOBLET

BUTTER SPREADER

BREAD & BUTTER PLATE

NAPKIN

SALAD PLATE

DINNER FORK

DINNER PLATE

TEASPOON
DINNER KNIFE

8

6) WAYS TO SLASH THE BUDGET

1. Limit your guest list

2. Use seasonal local flowers

3. Ask a family member or friend to DJ

4. Ask a family member or friend to be the Photographer/Videographer

5. If you need transportation, hire for a grand entrance or exit versus being on stand-by

6. Limit alcohol to beer, wine and a couple of specialty drinks

7. Do-it-yourself invitations/decorations

8. If using a venue, ask the site manager if there are other events that same day and possibly piggy back off their menu

7) DINNER STYLES

Buffet – Guests serve themselves
- Cost $
- Pros – Encourages mingling
- Cons – Long lines, things may get sloppy, the more choices higher the costs

Seated – Wait-staff brings plated dinners or family style platters to seated guests
- Cost $$
- Pros – Elegant and formal; everyone eats at the same time, it's easier to control the flow
- Cons – Restricts mingling, may require more wait-staff

Stations- Chef-manned stations
- Cost $$$
- Pros – Personalizes the dining experience
- Cons – Often the most expensive Option

8) SEATING

- **Cocktail** – High-top tables for two or four are great for the perimeter of the dance floor. Guests will tend to mingle.

- **Rectangular** – Gives the feel of being at a restaurant and less like a banquet.

- **Round** – Sense of intimacy, you can see and talk to everyone.

- **Square** – If you decide to have both rectangles and rounds, it can help to break things up.

Seating Option:

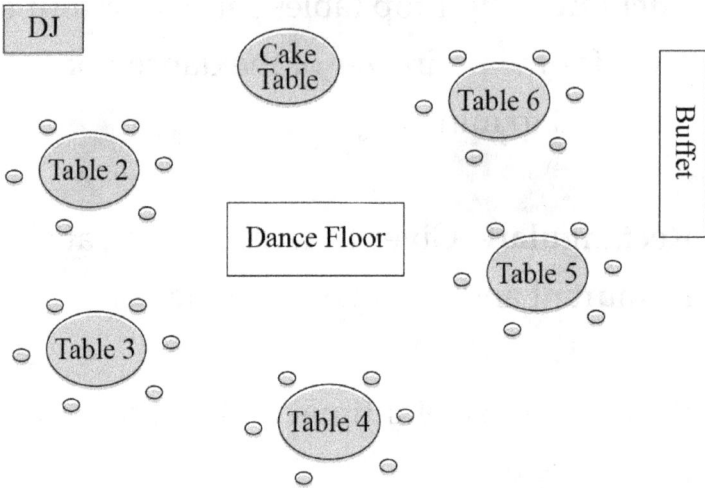

DJ

Cake Table

Table 6

Buffet

Table 2

Dance Floor

Table 5

Table 3

Table 4

Gift Table

Guest Book

Create your customized seating chart by visiting
http://www.weddingmapper.com/guests/demo_seating

9) SELECTION OF VENDORS

(When using vendors, be sure to have a signed contract with detailed information of services to be rendered.)

Cake Baker –

☐ Who will bake my cake?

☐ What are my filling choices?

☐ Do you customize cakes?

☐ How far in advance will the cake be prepared?

☐ How are your cakes priced?

☐ Are you licensed by the state?

Cake Baker: _____

Address: _____

Contact Person: _____

Deposit Due Date: _____

Final Payment Date: _____

Total Cost: _____

Set-up time: _____

Clean-up time: _____

Calligrapher –

☐   Are you a trained calligrapher?

☐   How are your rates calculated?

☐   What is the turn-around time?

☐   Do you have a portfolio that I may view?

Calligrapher: _____

Address: _____

Deposit Due Date: _____

Final Payment Date: _____

Total Cost: _____

Notes for services to be rendered:

_____

_____

_____

_____

_____

Caterer –

- ❑ What is your per person charge?
- ❑ How many menus are there to choose from?
- ❑ How many guests do you overestimate for?
- ❑ Do you allow food to be taken home?
- ❑ Will the gratuity be included in the final cost?
- ❑ How many hours are included in service?
- ❑ Is there an overtime charge?
- ❑ Do you provide staff to include bartenders?
- ❑ Is the set-up and cleanup included in the price?
- ❑ Do you provide chairs, flatware, linens, napkins and tables?
- ❑ Is there a charge to cut and serve the cake?
- ❑ Who will be the staff person in charge?
- ❑ How far in advance, will you need the final count?
- ❑ What payment arrangements do you require?

Caterer: _____

Address: _____

Contact Person: _____

Deposit Due Date: _____

Final Payment Date: _____

Total Cost: _____

Set-up time: _____

Clean-up time: _____

Menu:

Meats: _____

Vegetables: _____

Starch: _____

Bread: _____

Drinks: _____

Notes: _____

Entertainment –

❏ Will someone from your staff provide service as our Emcee?

❏ What are your set-up time requirements?

❏ How will you be dressed for the event?

❏ How far in advance do you need the playlist?

Entertainment Company: _____

Address: _____

Deposit Due Date: _____

Final Payment Date: _____

Total Cost: _____

Set-up Time: _____

End Time: _____

Notes for services to be rendered:

_____

_____

_____

_____

Florist –

❑ When do the flowers need to be ordered?

❑ How many people will be available to work my event?

❑ Do you have a portfolio that I may view?

❑ How will the flowers be stored once arranged?

❑ When will the flowers be delivered and set-up?

❑ Will you be able to preserve the flowers?

❑ Will the flowers be displayed in items that need to be returned?

Flower Company: _____

Address: _____

Deposit Due Date: _____

Final Payment Date: _____

Total Cost: _____

Set-up Time: _____

Total number of Flowers: _____

Types of Flowers:

_____

_____

_____

_____

Photographer/Videographer –

- ❑ Will the person I meet with, be the person that will shoot the event?

- ❑ What kind of lighting do you require?

- ❑ Will you have a backup camera?

- ❑ How many hours will you be available?

- ❑ How are your rates calculated?

- ❑ What is the minimum order requirement?

- ❑ What is the turn-around time on proofs?

- ❑ How will you be dressed for the event?

- ❑ Do you have budget conscience packets?

Photography/Videographer Company: _____

Address: _____

Deposit Due Date: _____

Final Payment Date: _____

Total Cost: _____

Set-up Time: _____

End Time: _____

Picture List:

_____

_____

_____

_____

Transportation –

- ❏ What kind of vehicles do you have for hire?

- ❏ How are your fees calculated?

- ❏ What time will the driver arrive?

- ❏ Will the driver stay in the vicinity of the event?

Transportation Company: _____

Address: _____

Driver Contact: _____

Deposit Due Date: _____

Final Payment Date: _____

Total Cost: _____

Pick-up Time: _____

Drop-off Time: _____

Notes for services to be rendered:

_____

_____

_____

_____

_____

Venues –

- [ ] What is the rental fee and hours available?

- [ ] What is the sitting and standing capacity?

- [ ] Is there a dressing room available?

- [ ] Does the venue require a membership to rent the facility?

- [ ] What are the requirements and restrictions?

- [ ] How much time is allowed for set-up and cleanup?

- [ ] What is the parking capacity?

- [ ] Are handicapped facilities available?

- [ ] How many outlets are there for Audio/Visual?

- [ ] What are the cleanup requirements?

- [ ] Do you have your own event coordinator?

- [ ] Do you allow outside alcohol?

Venue Site: _____

Address: _____

Phone Number: _____

Site Manager: _____

Date and Time Room Reserved: _____

Deposit Due Date: _____

Final Payment Date: _____

Total Cost: _____

Number of guests: _____

Set-up Instructions:

_____

_____

_____

_____

_____

10) ITINERARY

6 hour prior to the event
- Everyone should have something to eat

5 hour
- Start set up at your event location. If you are renting a venue, check-in with the site manager.

4 hour
- Apply linen to the tables
- Ensure food has been started or start earlier, if needed

3 hour
- The groom and his groomsmen will arrive at the designated location to get dressed. List Groom's cell phone number.

3 hour
- Start decorating
- Set the tables with flowers/place-settings

2 hour
- Provided you are the host, you will need to get dressed for the event

1 hour

- Set – up entertainment
- Set – up photos/videos

.30 min

- Verify everything is ready to go

.15 min

- Set-up cake
- Guests start arriving

.00min

- THE FUN BEGINS

Notes

Notes

1 hour

- Set – up entertainment
- Set – up photos/videos

.30 min

- Verify everything is ready to go

.15 min

- Set-up cake
- Guests start arriving

.00min

- THE FUN BEGINS

ACKNOWLEDGMENTS

The author wishes to express sincere appreciation to her family, friends and colleagues who encouraged and supported her along the way.

ABOUT THE AUTHOR

Latricia Bradley is a retired member of the United States military serving honorably for 21 years. During this time serving her country, Mrs. Bradley has earned both Accounting and Finance degrees to include a Master's in Business Administration. Mrs. Bradley is a certified event planner and wedding specialist who is now expanding her talent to photography, where she is currently pursuing a fifth degree.

www.ingramcontent.com/pod-product-compliance
Lightning Source LLC
Chambersburg PA
CBHW060751280326
41934CB00010B/2441